Masterpieces in The Museum of Primitive Art

Africa

Oceania

North America

Mexico

Central to South America

Peru

1965

Published by The Museum of Primitive Art
15 West 54th Street
New York 19, N. Y.
1965. All rights reserved

Printed in Switzerland
by Stämpfli+Cie, Berne.
Photographs by Charles Uht.
Jacket, maps and charts by Hiram Ash.

Library of Congress Card Number: 65-23544

The works illustrated in this book were created by artists of cultures still relatively unfamiliar to the western world, though they covered vast expanses of the world's surface – Africa, Oceania, North and South America; and evolved over many centuries – in the case of the Americas, nearly three thousand years.

Why "primitive"? It is true that some of the cultures whose products are illustrated here were, in many ways, of great sophistication: those, for instance, of Benin in Africa, or of the Inca and the Maya of the Americas. Even the artists of the simplest cultures have worked at the full stretch of their power – the Australian aborigines are an example – and have thus redeemed themselves from any possible charge of crudity or insensitivity. If we are to speak of these cultures, let alone these artists, as "primitive," we cannot mean that they are, in the popular sense of the word, crude or barbarous. "Primitive" can only be used here (as Lucy Mair defines it in her *Primitive Law*) to mean relatively undeveloped in technical processes and governmental institutions at the time of first contact with western culture. Today the word is used as a qualification, rather than a description, of these arts.

Indeed the actual usage itself may eventually become obsolete. This is not because we are likely to find a better portmanteau word – almost any other formula is more ponderous or less euphonious – but because of the growing comprehension that the art works themselves do not form an inchoate mass, but rather belong to separate and distinguishable styles, each with local habitation and name, and sometimes chronological position, as well as its own particular character and spirit.

Acquisition, preservation, exhibition and definition – these are the four goals The Museum of Primitive Art has set itself in its short career, which first took public form in 1957. It was then the only museum of its kind. Since that time at least one other has been established; some of the older natural history museums, with their extremely rich collections, have established curatorships in the subject; still others have revised their exhibitions to stress art rather than general ethnography. Probably more books on various areas of primitive art have been published in the last five years than in the two preceding decades: among them are over thirty-five from The Museum of Primitive Art alone.

Primitive art, then, is taking the place in public consciousness of great artistic traditions which it has always deserved. Its own traditions must be now summarized, though by necessity only with the greatest brevity.

Africa

(Numbers 1–31)

The art of Africa south of the Sahara is made up of many styles. Each of its primarily agricultural societies, necessarily organized in small economic and political units, developed a distinctive mode of expression intimately connected with a local culture.

As a whole, African art is characteristically bound up with religion and divination. Its larger figures portray ancestors, the mythical progenitors of the tribal group, or individuals of historical or social importance who often take on mythical stature. Its smaller figures include divinatory statuettes, protective spirits against misfortune, talismans against evil. Masks are essential to ritual and ceremony. They take part in the rites of initiation, in funeral dances and processions, in the magic festivals of sowing and harvest. On these occasions they invoke the forces which will protect the group against destruction and help it to increase. (This is the reason for the emphasis on natural and human fertility.) These forces belong to another world, therefore the inventiveness of the masks, their stylizations and expressive exaggerations. Most figures and masks have a communal function; many of them belong to the secret societies which provide the framework of the religious knowledge and social life of the community. As such they must be kept away from the uninitiates, which usually include all women.

But there is also an art of the court. In Ife and Benin, Dahomey and the Cameroons, reliefs and portrait heads were connected with the moral and secular authority of royal power. They also are more naturalistic than the great preponderance of African art that has its source in religion.

Useful objects also were embellished. Stools, neckrests, throwing knives, spoons, musical instruments, loom pulleys, doors of secret society houses and granaries carry emblematic heads and figures placing them under the protection of guardian spirits Here again art's aesthetic and social functions fuse to a common end.

The African sculptor is most often a part-time artist (except where he is attached to a court, as in Benin). He is also a farmer, and/or a "blacksmith" making implements and weapons. His status is always a special one, but the respect paid his special skills and knowledge is not always unmixed, because his craft touches on sacred and magic things that may render him dangerous. Like religious artists elsewhere, he must work within the limitations of traditional iconography and style; nevertheless he and his society value exceptional technical skill and formal sensitivity, and he is often an honored individual.

The typical art of Africa is sculpture; its characteristic medium, wood. The sculptor carves the trunk or branch fresh and green from the tree, first with an adze, then with a knife; he polishes with rough leaves, and brightens the surface with paint or darkens it with mud and vegetable oils. His raw material is always in the round, which is one reason why his sense of three-dimensional rhythm of mass and interval is acute and sure. He knows other techniques as well: stone, pottery, and, most widespread, both the solid and hollow casting of gold and bronze (or brass).

But the fact that most works have been in wood, and so have had a relatively short life, has reduced our knowledge of the history of African art to a minimum. The clay heads and figures from Nok in northern Nigeria go back to 1,000 B.C.; the finds in the Chad can be dated about the XV century; and the famous clay and bronze masterpieces of Ife (predecessor and teacher of Benin), belong to the XII and XIII centuries. But except possibly for some Dogon and Bambara figures, most sculpture in wood known to us today is no more than one hundred and fifty years old.

Oceania

(Numbers 32–61)

The vast flock of Pacific islands has long been the home of a very large number of diverse cultures, producing a range of art styles comparable in number to those of Africa or ancient America. This swarming inventiveness is all the more striking since in Oceania, even more than in Africa, the materials the artists used – primarily wood – were highly perishable, so that little has survived which was made before Euroepan infiltration began less than two centuries ago. The whole extant body of Oceanic art in all its splendid variety is thus the product of a remarkably limited time.

Its richness is partly due to the way in which Oceania was peopled. Studies of physical anthropology, archaeology, linguistics, oral traditions, art styles and material objects are building up a history which is very broad in some respects, though minutely detailed in others. It appears that the earliest immigrants – Tasmanians and Australoids – moved from southeast Asia along a land bridge into Australia before 10,000 B.C., bringing with them a very elementary material culture based on hunting. Around 3,000 B.C. dark-skinned agriculturalists (pre-Austronesians) came by sea to the area called Melanesia (New Guinea, the Admiralty and Solomon Islands, New Ireland and the New Hebrides). Later light-skinned immigrants (the Austronesians) were agriculturalists, fishermen and skilled navigators. They came in two major waves, one (1,500–700 B.C.) to parts of Melanesia and beyond; the second (500 B.C.–300 A.D.) to the small islands of Micronesia and Polynesia in a long-continued series of dispersions. In time interminglings of these populations, and comparative isolation in the areas they settled, generated local variations in belief and custom.

Most of the democratic Melanesian cultures were characterised by an avid quest for individual male grandeur in terms of headhunting prowess, wealth, political and (sometimes) artistic ability. The artist, a man with a special talent, worked part-time on commissions from individuals or groups. Recognition came because the higher the quality of his work, the greater was the resulting prestige of its ultimate owner. Communities exerted great efforts on ambitious architectural and ceremonial projects, usually dedicated to cults of ancestors, and mostly requiring an enormous paraphernalia. Melanesian art is consequently remarkable for dramatic fantasy (frequently on a grand scale) with variations on the human form.

The Polynesian cultures and their religious systems – formed by their own accounts through the imposition of invading groups on older populations – were often intensely hierarchical. In Tahiti, for instance, semi-divine rulers controlled aristocratic landowners who in turn directed a subservient laboring class. The professional craftsmen (including artists) occupied an intermediate place between landowners and plebians. Among the New Zealand Maori, however, the artist ranked among the "tohunga," a class of experts of all kinds, including the priesthood. Something of the formality of the societies is reflected in Polynesian art's exquisite craftsmanship and reliance on patterns (often abstracted from the human figure). A few statues from Mangareva have rare naturalism; oftener Polynesian figure sculpture (Maori, Marquesan, Hawaiian) reflects in a polished way the ferocious conventions of Melanesian art.

Micronesian art is, as befits its historic relationships, somewhat Polynesian in its spare elegance; it is also as sparse as might be expected from this relatively impoverished, marginal area. The character of art from Australia, Oceania's other marginal area, is totally different: its largely religious content is expressed in a multiplicity of enigmatic, geometric symbols or imaginative stylizations from the natural world.

North America

(Numbers 62–72)

The arts of North America are many and varied. From the early Eskimo cultures around the Bering Strait to the productions of the Plains Indians, they cover a huge geographical area and a period of several millenia. The range in media is equally large: brightly painted wooden pieces of the Northwest Coast, finely finished stone objects from the Midwest, carefully engraved shells from the Southeast, painted hides of the Plains, weavings of the Southwest, to name but a few. Yet the North American Indian never achieved the level of civilization attained in Mexico and Peru. Technically and ideologically less developed, their history and their art forms are more illusive and more perishable. Certain areas, particularly in the southern United States, were undeniably influenced by the late, great developments in Mexico.

Mexico

(Numbers 80–103)

To the archaeologist, pre-Columbian Mexican art supplies clues to the vast story of life in this hemisphere, laboriously unearthed, painstakingly put together. To the lovers of the unknown, it presents visions of horror and grandeur, pantheons of strange gods, unheard of religions, unimaginable events. Of the uninitiated its immediate inaccessibility demands attention and thought. For the connoisseur it offers twenty-five hundred years of artistic traditions uninfluenced by the formal values of western art. The art of Mexico can be huge, massive, hieratic, or small, personal, intimate. It can serve purposes of state, the demands of death, the ritual of sacrifice. It is awe inspiring. It can be charming. Its history is one of accumulation and growth; separate areas of superior development and invention influencing, or contributing to, the whole; other areas evolving chiefly within themselves.

The beginnings of "official" art in Mexico are found among the Olmec of the Gulf Coast (c. 800 B.C.). The first high civilization of Middle America, it produced an area for ritual activity, the building, maintenance and use of which involved, to some extent, almost all the art forms. Juxtaposed pyramidal structures and open courts, their periodic renewal and enlargement, monolithic carved stelae, votive or funerary offerings as an integral part of the complex are all basic to centuries of Mexican growth, as are the high value placed on greenstones of various kinds, the depiction of personages in ceremonial regalia, and the use of small mask forms. Olmec influences extend into the Valley of Mexico which subsequently saw the rise of Teotihuacan, into the Valley of Oaxaca where Monte Alban was to flourish, and, its main force shattered, the last Olmec vestiges disappear where the Maya culture is thought to begin, in highland Guatemala.

Teotihuacan became the next important artistic impulse. The Valley of Mexico had been the early site of numerous and inventive ceramic complexes and to its cultural superiority Teotihuacan was to give final glory. Elegant, sophisticated and of great power, its art was highly esteemed and echoed throughout Mexico; the art of Monte Alban was more regional and the Maya were on their own independent and incomparable path, producing what many consider the greatest art of the pre-Colombian world. Teotihuacan was the first of these three cultures to disappear, the city destroyed (c. 600 A.D.), yet its influence remained strong and in legend it became the home of the gods. By the tenth century, the Toltecs controlled the Valley, Monte Alban had been abandoned and the Mixtecs were the growing power in Oaxaca. To the south, the Maya, too, had run their course and they were to witness direct Toltec intervention.

The Mixtec were innovators and gifted artisans, having had enough time to establish their own styles, whereas the Valley of Mexico traditions still imposed themselves on those who settled there. Among them were the Aztec, a backward, barbaric tribe when they first entered the Valley in the thirteenth century: their climb to power was based on great warrior ability, and their astonishing acculturation on a capacity for assimilation, primarily of the vast monumentality of the Valley of Mexico heritage, and the wealth of attentive and beautifully produced Mixtec forms. The Mixteca-Puebla styles which developed as the Mixtec expanded north were by far the strongest of immediately-pre-Aztec Mexico and continued to maintain strength as they influenced them. Numbers of other distinct styles, localized developments not unrelated to the whole yet best seen independently, of an independence often imposed by racial difference, geographic isolation, or a highly favored and specific vision – the Huaxtec of northern Veracruz, the classic area of Tajin, the Remojadas ceramics, the Colima, Nayarit and Jalisco styles of the Pacific Coast, the Mezcala productions of Guerrero – all add to the variety and character of Mexican art.

Central to South America
(Numbers 73–79)

Costa Rica, Panama, Colombia and Peru have yielded the largest quantity of pre-Columbian gold objects; so vast was the amount of gold taken from them at the time of the Conquest that the economy of much of Europe was affected by it. The gold styles of Costa Rica are those identified mainly with the Diquís and Chiriqui regions; in Panama there are the Coclé and Veraguas styles; in Colombia many styles are known, Calima, Tolima, Quimbaya, Sinú, Tairona and Muisca among them. A tradition of fine stone carving is found in Costa Rica, particularly in the Nicoya Peninsula and Central Plateau areas, the most southerly regions to be extensively influenced by Mexican culture. The Caribbean area, culturally defined from Cuba in the north through northern Venezuela and the Guianas in the south, also yields traces of influence from Mexico and Central America.

Peru
(Numbers 104–134)

The distinctive geography of the Central Andean region – the narrow and extremely arid coast, next to which rise the Andes, high and abrupt – makes it, as a rule, inhabitable only in certain specific valley areas. A considerable degree of isolation results, and ancient Peruvian art is marked by the spirit of that isolation, each separate region tending to develop its own characteristic style. Easy flow between areas does not generally occur; influence, when it exists, is a matter of considerable selection. Change and innovation are not characteristic of pre-Columbian Peruvian art; it is exceptionally traditional. But in time with the lessening of regional holds, styles become broader, less distinct, culminating in the universality of Inca art.

The earliest great art style appears in Peru about 1,000 B.C. Chavin art is voluminous and weighty. Its nucleus is in the north – at the highland temple site of Chavin de Huántar, and in the tiny Cupisnique valley on the coast – but it is by no means confined there. Chavinoid remains are found down the coast and, below the Paracas Peninsula, the earliest southern style, Paracas Cavernas, is strongly Chavinoid in character. The Paracas ceramics are smaller, lighter and more brightly colored than those of the north. Distinctions between the art of the northern and southern coasts are already apparent at this time: in the north, round, sculptural volumes and mono-chrome color preferences; in the south, less form and more and brighter color. These differences remain throughout later developments.

With the lessening of the Chavinoid hold throughout Peru the first series of well developed, truly regional styles appear. Localized particularly in the coastal valleys, the strongest were the Mochica in the north and the Nazca in the south. The Mochica style is reflective of both the agressive and dynamic nature of its makers as well as the great Chavinoid sculptural tradition on which it was, somewhat distantly, based. The Nazca, more directly tied to its immediate Paracas antecedents, is less open and more involuted in style, relying heavily on intricate symbolic designs and carefully worked surface for its most direct appeal.

In the centuries after 500 A.D. the highland valleys of the south produced a new and vital art. Named for the extensive site of Tiahuanaco on the shores of Lake Titicaca, the "Tiahuanaco style" seems actually to be a complex of very closely related yet separate styles which spread through the highlands to the coast. Few areas remain untouched by it, but the south-central coastal region is perhaps the most important "Coast Tiahuanaco" area. Highland Tiahuanaco art is rectilinear, severe and strong, whereas the coast styles are rounder, lighter, more imaginative.

As the Tiahuanaco influences disappear (after about 1,000 A.D.) local developments gradually re-emerge, yet not on the same artistic level as its first occurrence, nor with the same intense regionalism. Larger areas are involved: on stretches of the north coast the Chimu style flourishes, as do the Chancay on the central coast, and the Ica in the south. Although each has its own distinctive local character, they all share a certain aesthetic disinterest, apparent in such things as technical carelessness or poverty of idea. Of them all, the Chancay succeeds most in its remarkable spontaneity.

Coincident with these developments on the coast, Inca art began to evolve in the highlands. Grounded in the Tiahuanaco tradition, it was lean, simple, and functional, and virtually mass produced. The Inca conquests, which began in the 1430's and embraced during a ninety-year period a territory of 350,000 square miles, provided ample opportunity for the use and dissemination of their art forms. Assimilative of ideal and technique, however, the art of the period is greatly enriched by interacting Inca and local styles. The process was all quickly ended with the arrival of the conquering Spaniards in 1532.

It is from these backgrounds that the 135 objects shown in the following pages – a fraction of the Museum's collection, though a significant one – have been drawn. None are the work of living societies. Today, first under the impact of western culture, and then owing to its adoption in the place of older structures, the indigenous cultures of Africa and Oceania are almost as extinct as those of pre-Columbian America. But such works as these remain as their monuments, and in many cases as their chief contribution to the record of human achievement.

Frontispiece: Detail of shirt section in tapestry weave with stylized feline design. Peru, Central or South Coast: Tiahuanaco. Wool, cotton, 19⁷/₈″ wide. 56.195. (Photo Nickolas Muray)

AFRICA

Facing Africa section: Pectoral representing human face mask. Nigeria, Benin: Bini. Ivory, iron, copper, stone, 9³/₈″ high. 58.100

1. Hermaphrodite. Mali, Bandiagara: Dogon (Tellem). Wood, 82⁷/₈″ high. 58.97

2. Ritual object. Mali: Dogon. Wood, 17¹/₈″ high. 62.156

3. Mask (satimbe). Mali: Dogon. Wood, 43⁵/₈″ high. 61.5

4. Ancestral figure. Mali, Bougouni district: Bambara. Wood, 48⁵/₈″ high. 59.110

5. Female antelope headdress. Upper Volta: Kurumba. Wood, traces of white and red paint, 39¹/₈″ high. 63.41

6. Head. Guinea: (prehistoric). Stone, 10¹/₄″ high. 60.35

7. Headdress, Simo secret society (nimba). Guinea: Baga. Wood, 46¹/₂″ high. 56.261

8. Mask, Poro secret society. Liberia: Dan. Wood, 8⁵/₈″ high. 57.109

9. Mask. Liberia, Cape Palmas region: Grebo. Wood, white and blue paint, 27¹/₂″ high. 56.217

10. Rhythm pounder (déblé). Ivory Coast, Korhogo district, Lataha village: Senufo, Tiembara fraction. Wood, 42¹/₂″ high. 58.7

11. Bird headdress (porpianong). Ivory Coast: Senufo. Wood, red and white paint, 59⁵/₈″ high. 60.57

12. Standing male figure. Ivory Coast: Baule. Wood, traces of coloring, beads, 21³/₄″ high. 60.84

13. Ancestral figure. Ivory Coast: Baule. Wood, glass beads, white paint, 18¹/₈″ high. 56.365

14. Pendant in form of a turtle. Ghana: Ashanti. Gold, 4″ high. 60.36

15. Goldweight in form of a chameleon. Ghana: Ashanti. Bronze, 3⁵/₈″ long. 57.235

16. Pendant in form of an animal mask. Ivory Coast: Baule. Gold, 3³/₈″ high, 3⁵/₈″ wide. 56.398

17. Ancestral figure. Ivory Coast: Baule or Guro. Wood, white paint, beads, 25⁷/₈″ high. 59.23

18. Funerary head. Ghana: Ashanti. Clay, 12³/₈″ high. 59.241

19. Horn player. Nigeria, Benin: Bini. Bronze, 24⁷/₈″ high. 57.255

20. Plaque. Nigeria, Benin: Bini. Bronze, 19¹/₂″ high, 16¹/₂″ wide. 57.231

21. Shango cult figure. Nigeria: Yoruba. Wood, traces of red and black paint, 28$^1/_2$" high. 56.220

22. Guardian spirit. Nigeria: Western Ijo. Wood, traces of black and white paint, 25$^1/_2$" high. 60.128. Gift of the Matthew T. Mellon Foundation

23. Ancestral figure. Cameroun: Bamum. Wood, 34" high. 61.256

24. Mask. Congo (Brazzaville): Bakwele. Wood, white, rust and umber paint, 20$^3/_4$" high. 56.218

25. Reliquary figure (naja). Gabon: Bakota. Wood, metal, 30$^3/_8$" high. 61.247

26. Ghost mask. Gabon: Ogowe River area. Wood, red, white and black paint, 11$^3/_8$" high. 56.403. Gift of Mr. Eliot Elisofon

27. Reliquary figure. Gabon: Fang. Wood, metal, 25$^1/_4$" high. 61.284

28. Reliquary head (the Great Bieri). Gabon: Fang. Wood, metal, 18$^1/_4$" high. 61.283

29. Stool. Congo (Leopoldville): Baluba. Wood, blue and white beads, 23$^1/_4$" high. 61.47

30. Mask, Bwame secret society. Congo (Leopoldville): Warega. Ivory, 8$^1/_2$" high. 61.285

31. Mask, Kifwebe secret society. Congo (Leopoldville): Northwestern Baluba. Wood, black and white paint, 14$^5/_8$" high. 56.56

OCEANIA

32. Sacred stone (churinga). Australia, Northern Territory: Pidgentara. Stone, 12" long. 56.73

33. Mask (eharo). New Guinea, Papuan Gulf, Orokolo: Elema. Painted bark cloth over cane, fibre, 28$^3/_4$" high. 58.309

34. Ceremonial board (gope). New Guinea, Papuan Gulf, Wapo Creek. Painted wood, 50$^3/_4$" high. 62.83

35. Mother and child. New Guinea, Lorentz River, Komor: Asmat. Painted wood, fibre, 55$^1/_8$" high. 61.52

36. Shield. New Guinea, Eilanden River: Asmat. Painted wood, 84$^5/_8$" high. 56.267

37. Ceremonial board (malu). New Guinea, middle Sepik River area: Chawos. Wood, 74$^1/_2$" high. 56.320

38. Flute ornament. New Guinea, middle Sepik River area, Kwoiwut: Chawos. Wood, bamboo, shells, 62$^3/_4$" high. 61.266

39. Suspension hook. New Guinea, middle Sepik River: Iatmul. Wood, paint, 53$^3/_4$" high. 61.280

40.a Canoe prow. New Guinea, middle Sepik River: Iatmul. Wood, shells, 71$^1/_2$" long. 55.1

40.b Detail of 40.a

41. Mask from house-gable. New Guinea, Sepik District, Chambri Lake area, Sangriman. Basketry, feathers, paint, tusks, 67″ high. 65.26

42. Ancestral figure (yipwon). New Guinea, Sepik District, upper Karawari River. Wood, Basketry, 86″ high. 65.37

43. Ancestral figure. New Guinea, lower Sepik River, Singrin village. Wood, 77 1/2″ high. 59.12

44. Canoe prow ornament. New Ireland, Lemusmus district. Painted wood, 21 3/4″ high. 58.323

45. Slit-drum head. New Hebrides, Ambrym. Wood, 61 1/4″ high. 59.281

46. Finial head. New Hebrides, Malekula: Big Nambas. Fernwood, 41″ high. 60.107

47. Bowl. New Hebrides. Wood, 39 3/4″ high. 61.1

48. Ear ornament. Polynesia, Marquesas Islands. Ivory, 3″ long. 62.30a

49. Ear ornament. Polynesia, Marquesas Islands. Ivory, 3″ long. 62.30b

50. Figure. Polynesia, Marquesas Islands. Bone, 4 3/8″ high. 63.59

51. Shield. Solomon Islands, Rubiana. Basketry, mother-of-pearl, paint, 33 1/4″ high. 59.111

52. Housepost figure. Polynesia, New Zealand: Maori. Wood, 43 1/8″ high. 58.240

53. Female figure (moai kavakava). Polynesia, Easter Island. Wood, bone and obsidian eyes, 17 1/8″ high. 58.98

54. Ceremonial paddle (rapa). Polynesia, Easter Island. Wood, 32 7/8″ high. 56.309

55. Figure of a god (Rongo?). Polynesia, Gambier Islands, Mangareva. Wood, 38 1/4″ high. 57.91

56. Sacred drum (pahu-ra). Polynesia, Austral Islands, Raivavai? Wood, shark skin, cord, 51 3/8″ high. 57.251

57. Pendant: female figure (niho-palaoa). Polynesia, Hawaii. Bone, 2 3/8″ high. 61.35

58. Pendant: female figure. Polynesia, Tonga Islands, Haapai group; collected in Fiji. Ivory, 5 1/4″ high. 57.108

59. Turtle effigy bowl. Polynesia, Fiji Islands. Wood, 22 1/4″ long. 60.83

60. Coconut grater. Micronesia, Caroline Islands, Nukuoro. Wood, 22 1/4″ long. 56.93

61. Navigational chart. Micronesia, Marshall Islands. Rattan, fibre, 36 1/4″ by 43 1/4″. 63.57. Gift of the Estate of Kay Sage Tanguy

NORTH AMERICA

62. Mask. United States, Alaska, Kuskokwim River: Eskimo. Wood, paint, feathers, string, 45 1/2″ high. 61.39

63. Dead man mask. United States, Alaska: Tlingit. Wood, paint, metal, leather, 13 5/8" high. 56.330

64. Standing female figure. Canada, British Columbia: Kwakiutl. Wood, 50" high. 56.205

65. Kneeling figure. United States. Tennessee, Humphreys County, Duck River: Mississippi. Stone, 26 1/4" high. 57.1

66. Gorget, rattlesnake design. United States, Tennessee, Hamilton County, Chickamuaga Creek. Shell, 4 1/4" high. 56.389

67. Bannerstone. United States, Ohio? Stone, 2 3/4" high. 56.227

68. Bannerstone. United States, Missouri, Boone County. Stone, 3 7/8" high. 64.17

69. Mask. United States, Tennessee, Tennessee River, Williams Island. Shell, 6 3/4" high. 58.77

70. War god. United States, New Mexico: Zuni. Wood, traces of paint, 29 3/4" high. 64.8. Gift of Mr. and Mrs. Raymond Wielgus

71. Blanket. United States, Arizona: Navajo. Wood, 80 × 55 3/4". 64.27

72. Buffalo robe, woman's design. United States, Wyoming: Arapaho. Hide, paint, 73 × 80". 64.50

CENTRAL TO SOUTH AMERICA

73. Figure of a god. Jamaica: Taino. Wood, shell inlay, 27" high. 56.180

74. Standing figure. Costa Rica, Central Plateau, Reventazón area? Stone, 34 3/4" high. 56.279

75. Pectoral. Costa Rica, Chiríqui area, Puerto Gonzalez Viquez. Gold, pyrite, 6" high. 63.4

76. Plaque. Panama: Coclé? Gold, 7 1/8" high. 58.18

77. Pendant figure. Colombia: Tairona. Gold, 3 1/8" high. 61.30

78. Axe-form pendant. Colombia: Tolima. Gold, 7 1/8" high. 57.46

79. Lid for a pottery vessel. Colombia: Quimbaya. Gold, 5 3/8" high. 57.158

MEXICO

80. Mask. Valley of Mexico, Tlatilco. Clay, paint, 5 1/4" high. 63.31

81. Incised celt. Tabasco? Olmec. Jadeite, 14 3/8" long. 56.52

82. Warrior vessel. Colima. Clay, 14 3/8" high. 57.9

83. Acrobat vessel. Colima. Clay, 9 1/4" high. 62.167

84. Standing figure. Guerrero: Mezcala. Stone, 13 3/4" high. 59.266. Gift of Mr. Luis de Hoyos

85. Standing figure. Valley of Mexico: Teotihuacan. Stone, 16 1/8" high. 57.201

86. Bridge and spout jar. Oaxaca: Monte Alban I. Clay, 13" high. 56.238

87. Effigy vessel. Oaxaca: Monte Alban II. Clay, 7 3/8" high. 61.32

88. Standing figure. Veracruz: Huaxtec. Stone, 34 3/8" high. 56.291

89. Hacha. Veracruz: Tajin (Classic Veracruz). Stone, 20 7/8" high. 56.297

90. Palma. Veracruz: Tajin (Classic Veracruz). Stone, 20 1/8" high. 56.284

91. Palma. Veracruz: Tajin (Classic Veracruz). Stone, 18 5/8" high. 56.283

92. Coyote? Veracruz: Remojadas. Clay, paint, 20" high. 60.185

93. Smiling head. Veracruz: Remojadas. Clay, 8 3/4" high. 57.191

94. Seated figure. Tabasco, found near the Guatemalan border: Maya. Wood, 14" high. 62.172

95. Standing figure whistle. Campeche, said to be from the Island of Uaymil: Maya. Clay, paint, 11 1/2" high. 61.72

96. Double-chambered vessel. Said to have come from coastal Campeche: Maya. Clay, 11 7/8" high. 62.46

97. Stela. Guatemala, Piedras Negras: Maya. Stone, traces of paint, 96" high. 63.163

98. Wall panel. Mexico, Campeche: Maya. Limestone, paint, 35" high, 34 1/2" wide. 62.102

99. Chac head. Yucatan, Chichen Itza, found in the Temple of the Little Heads: Maya-Toltec. Stone, 13 3/4" high. 57.66

100. Tlaloc mask. Oaxaca or Puebla: Mixteca-Puebla. Stone, 5 1/2" high. 62.169

101. Quetzalcoatl. Valley of Mexico: Aztec. Stone, 22 1/2" high. 57.242

102. Rattlesnake. Valley of Mexico: Aztec. Stone, 13 1/2" high. 57.2

103. Xipe Totec. Puebla: Aztec. Clay, paint, 56 3/4" high. 63.162

PERU

104. Cup. North Coast? Cupisnique. Stone, 3 1/2" high. 64.9

105. Stirrup spout jar. North Coast, Chicama valley? Cupisnique. Clay, 9 5/8" high. 59.4

106. Bridge and spout effigy vessel. North Coast, Virú valley? Gallinaso? Clay, 8 3/8" high. 59.187

107. Trophy head double spout vessel. South Coast: Paracas Necropolis. Clay, 7 1/4" high. 62.166

108. Drum. South Coast: Paracas Cavernas. Clay, resin paint, 15" high. 63.87

109. Ornament. Peru, South Coast: Nazca. Gold, 4⁷/₈″ high. 57.61a

110. Ornament. Peru, South Coast: Nazca. Gold, 4⁷/₈″ high. 57.61b

111. Headdress ornament or pin. South Coast: Nazca. Gold, 13³/₄″ high. 52.222a

112. Drum. South Coast: Nazca. Clay, paint, 17³/₄″ high. 64.4. Gift of Mr. and Mrs. Raymond Wielgus

113. Figure. South Coast, said to be from the Nazca valley. Stone, 13″ high. 60.138

114. Necklace. North Coast: Mochica. Gold, 49″ long. 56.396

115. Head jar. North Coast: Mochica. Clay, 4⁵/₈″ high. 61.19

116. Stirrup spout effigy vessel. North Coast: Mochica. Clay, 4⁵/₈″ high. 56.247

117. Incense vessel. Bolivia: Tiahuanaco. Clay, paint, 10¹/₈″ high. 63.3

118. Pendant. Central or South Coast: Coast Tiahuanaco. Shell, gold, wood, stone, 1⁵/₈″ high. 57.282

119. Standing figure. South Highlands: Tiahuanaco. Stone, 18³/₈″ high. 59.8

120. Fragment of an effigy vessel. Central or South Coast: Coast Tiahuanaco. Clay, paint, 9″ high. 61.14

121. Figure. Central Highlands: Huaraz. Stone, 25″ high. 60.102

122. Standing figure. Central Coast: Chancay. Clay, paint, 25″ high. 60.22

123. Shirt. Central Coast: Chancay. Wool, cotton, 49⁷/₈ × 70″. 61.75

124. Funerary mask. North Coast, Lambayeque valley, Batan Grande: Chimu. Gold, 28³/₄″ wide. 57.161

125. Ear spool. North Coast: Chimu. Gold, 3¹/₂″ diameter. 57.164a

126. Ear spool. North Coast: Chimu. Gold, 3¹/₂″ diameter. 57.165b

127. Ear spool. North Coast: Chimu. Gold, 4¹/₈″ high. 58.74

128. Shrine figure? North Coast: Chimu. Wood, 28¹/₄″ high. 58.257

129. Monkey eating fruit(?). North Coast: Chimu. Wood, 11⁵/₈″ high. 56.114

130. Shrine figure? North Coast? Inca. Wood, paint, 29¹/₂″ high. 56.115

131. Tomb post in the form of an agricultural implement (detail). South Coast, Ica valley: Inca. Wood, resin paint, 75³/₄″ high. 62.4

132. Standing figure. South Highlands, Cuzco area? Gold, 2³/₈″ high. 62.159

133. Effigy face beaker. Central or South Coast: Inca. Silver, 9³/₄″ high. 63.106

134. Plate? South Highlands? Stone, 11¹/₂″ diameter. 58.223

Africa

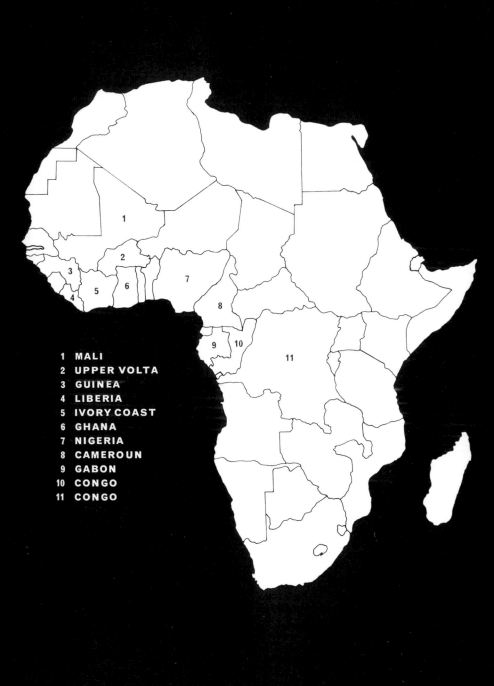

1 MALI
2 UPPER VOLTA
3 GUINEA
4 LIBERIA
5 IVORY COAST
6 GHANA
7 NIGERIA
8 CAMEROUN
9 GABON
10 CONGO
11 CONGO

1

4

6

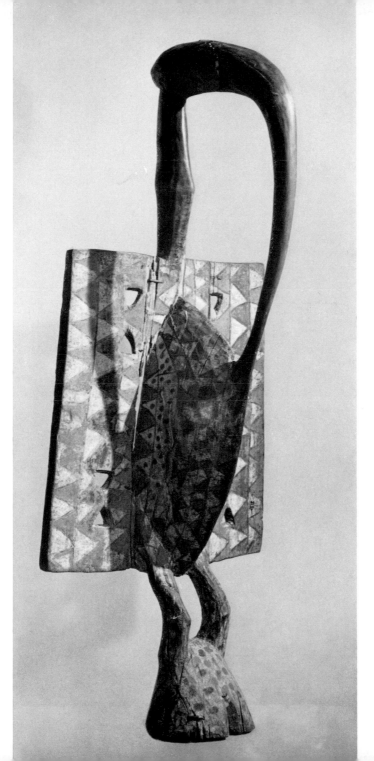

12

13

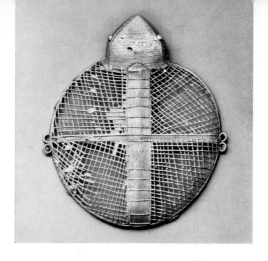

14

15

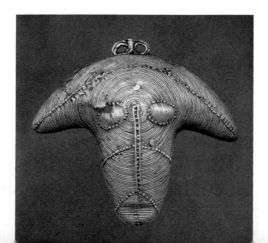

16

Oceania

Micronesia

ATOR EQUATOR EQUATOR EQUATOR EQUATOR EQUATOR EQUATOR EQUATOR EQUATOR EQUATOR EQUATOR EQUATOR EQUA

WUVULU

NEW IRELAND

SOLOMON ISLANDS

NEW GUINEA

Melanesia

FIJI ISLANDS

NEW HEBRIDES

TONGA ISLANDS

AUSTRALIA

NEW ZEALAND

TASMANIA

HAWAII

EQUATOR EQUATOR EQUATOR EQUATOR EQUATOR EQUATOR EQUATOR EQUATOR EQUATOR EQUATOR EQUATOR EQUATOR EQU

Polynesia

MARQUESAS ISLANDS

MANGAREVA

AUSTRAL ISLANDS

EASTER ISLAND •

34

38

40a

40b

43

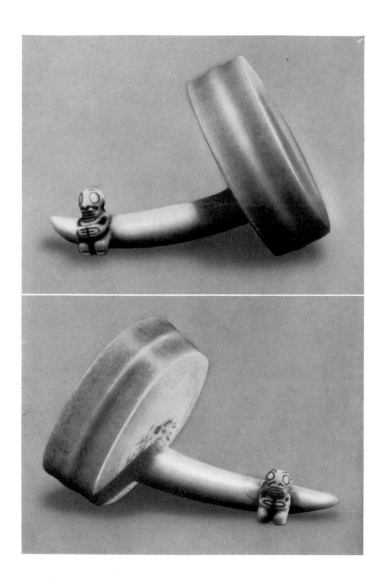

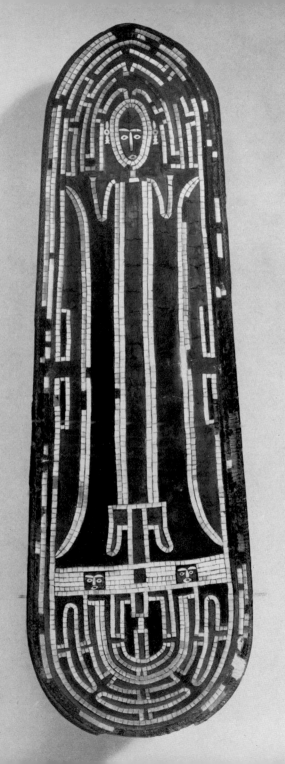

51

57a

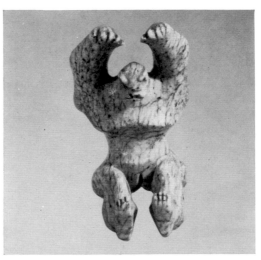

57b

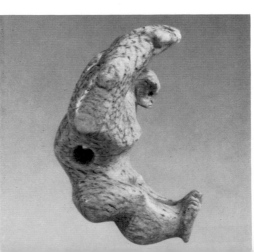

57c

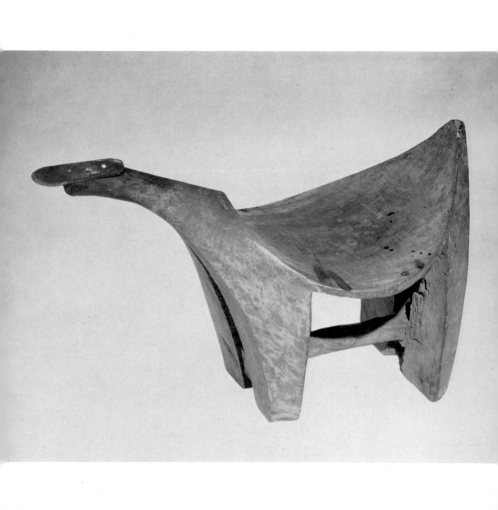

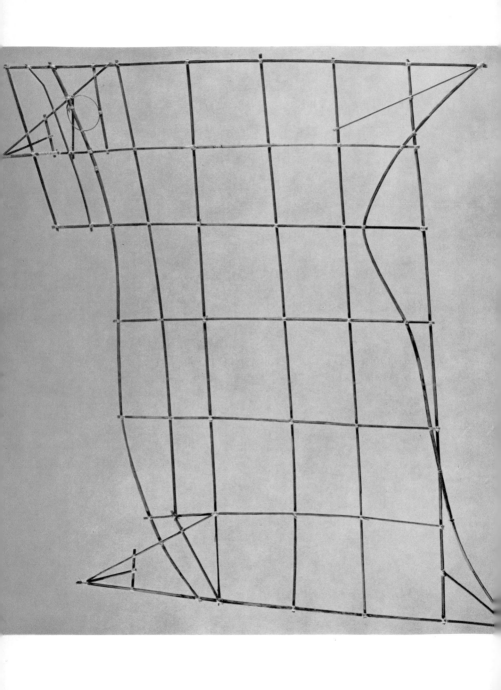

North America

(including Central to South America)

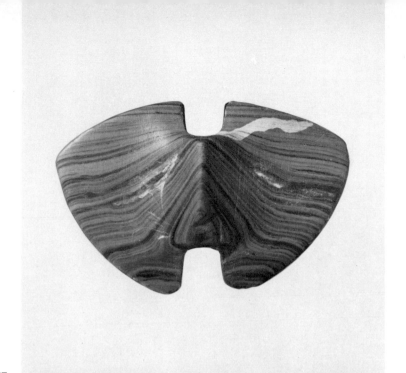

67

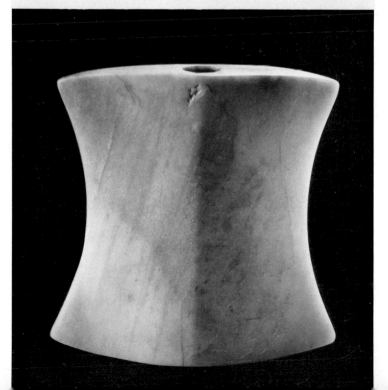

68

70

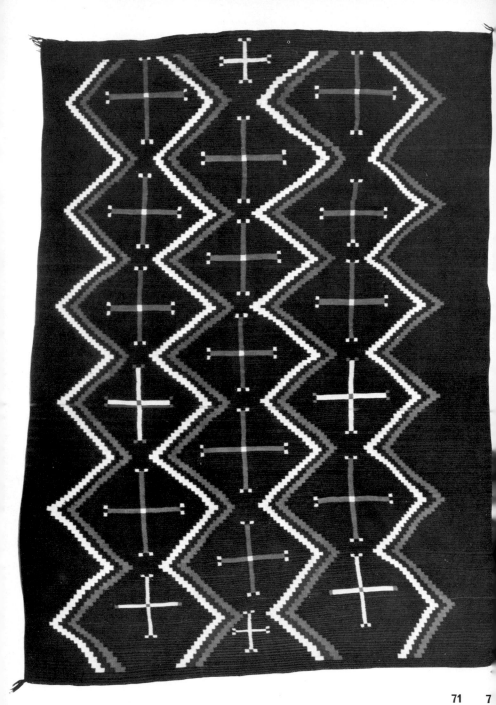

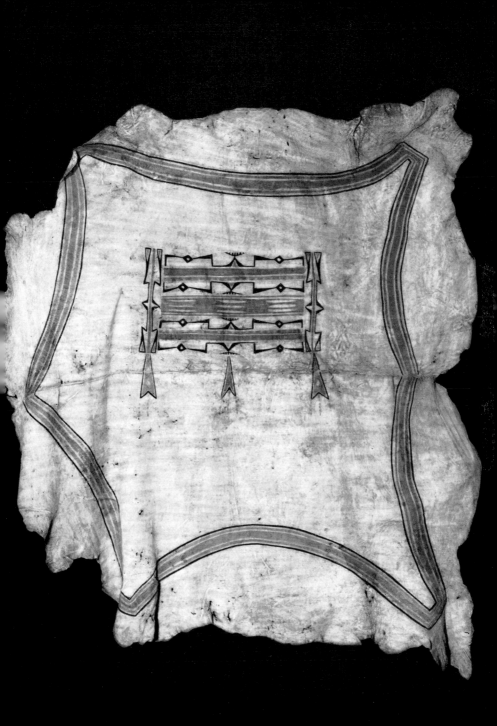

73

74

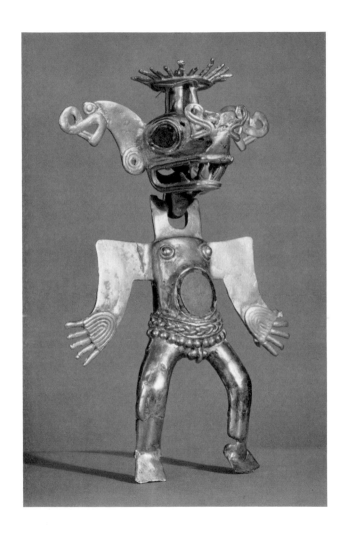

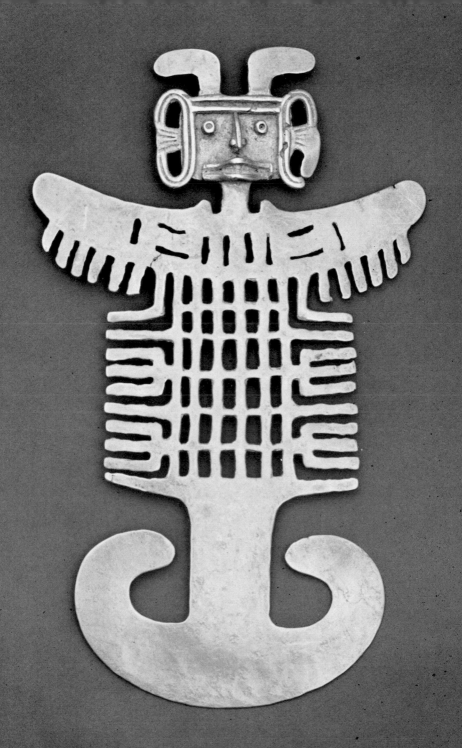

Mexico

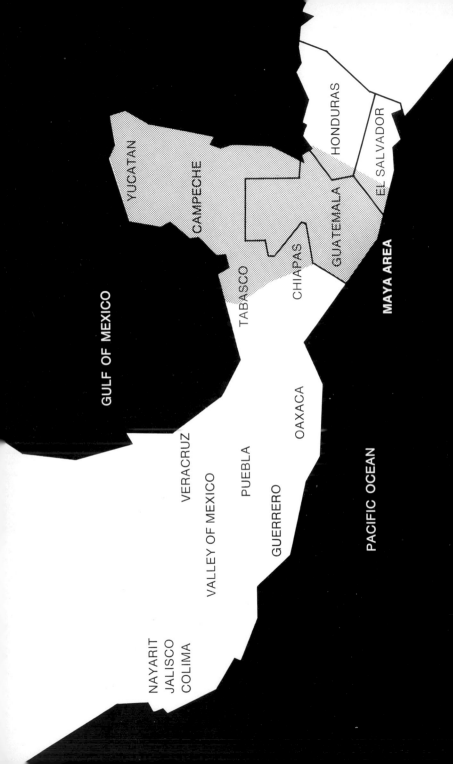

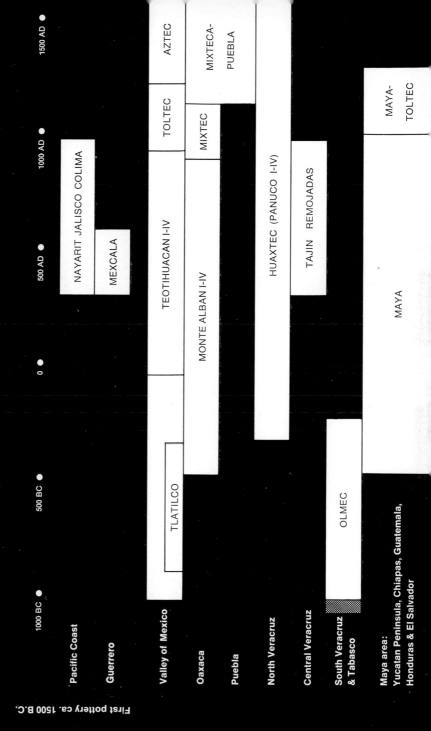

First pottery ca. 1500 B.C.

	1000 BC	500 BC	0	500 AD	1000 AD	1500 AD

Pacific Coast — NAYARIT JALISCO COLIMA

Guerrero — MEXCALA

Valley of Mexico — TLATILCO / TEOTIHUACAN I-IV / TOLTEC / AZTEC

Oaxaca — MONTE ALBAN I-IV / MIXTEC / MIXTECA-PUEBLA

Puebla — MIXTECA-PUEBLA

North Veracruz — HUAXTEC (PANUCO I-IV)

Central Veracruz — TAJIN REMOJADAS

South Veracruz & Tabasco — OLMEC

Maya area:
Yucatan Peninsula, Chiapas, Guatemala,
Honduras & El Salvador — MAYA / MAYA-TOLTEC

81

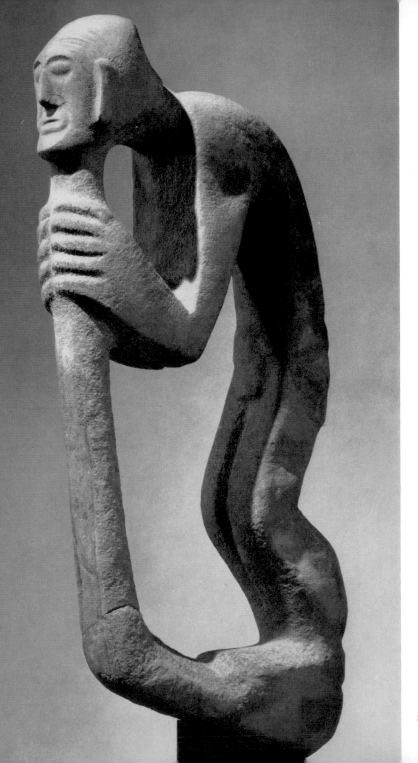

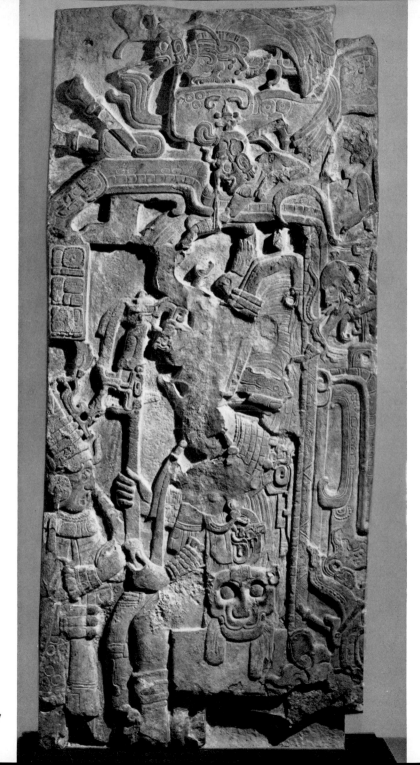

97

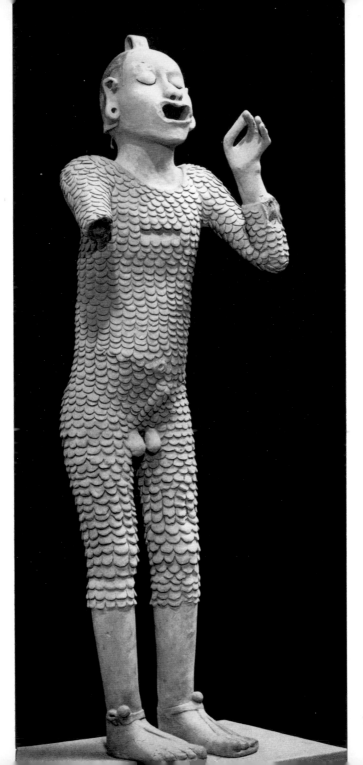

Peru

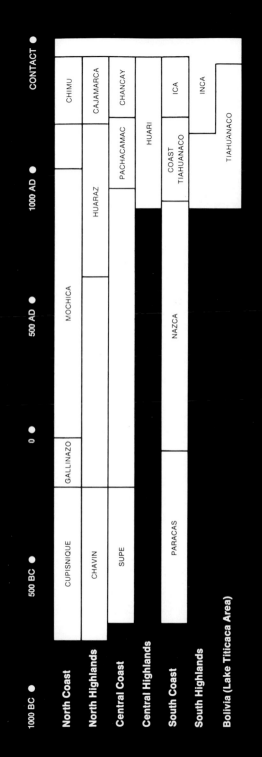

111

119

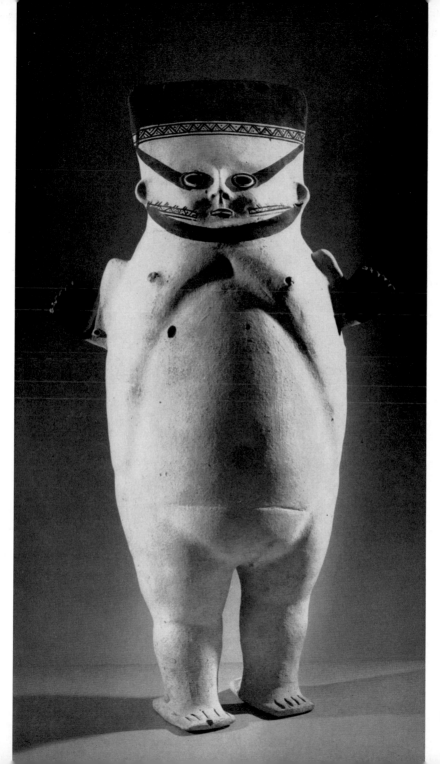

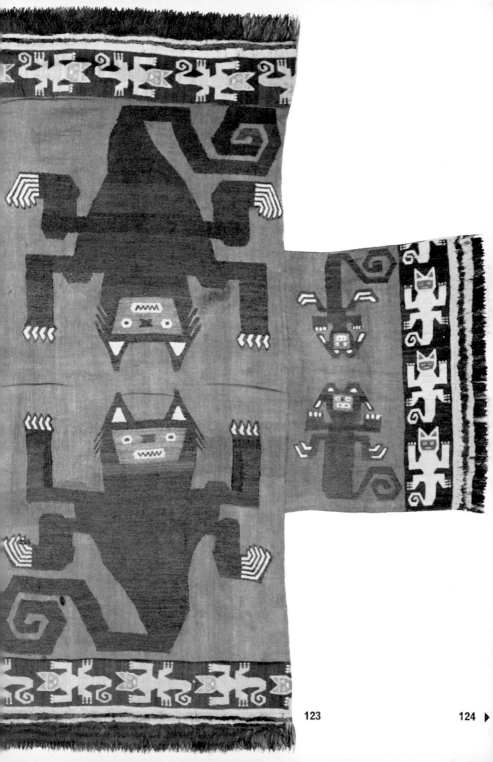

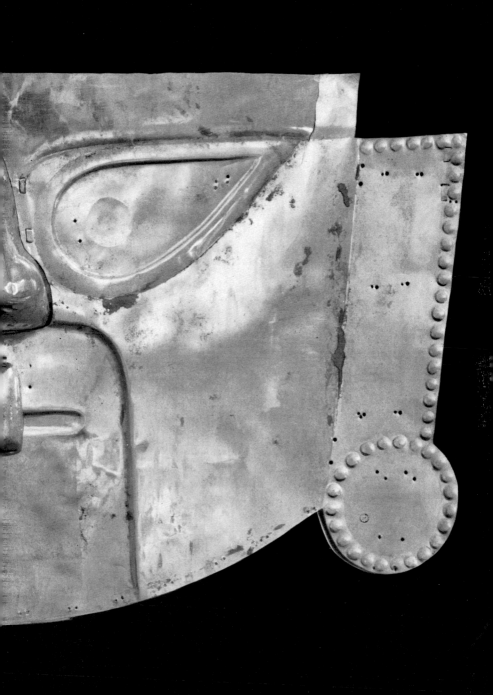

◀ 125
◀ 126
◀ 127

128

129a

129b